Pick a Plant!

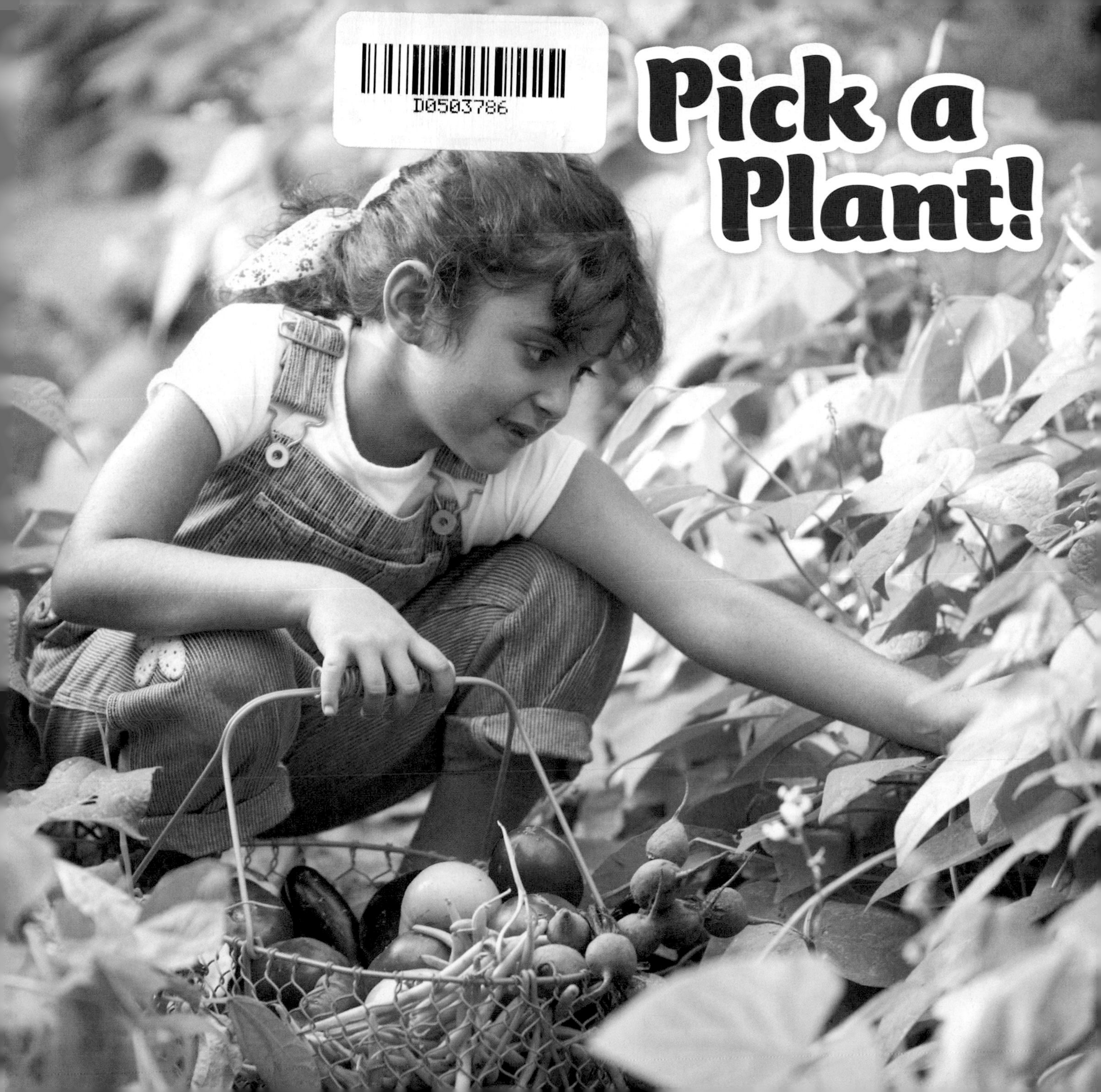

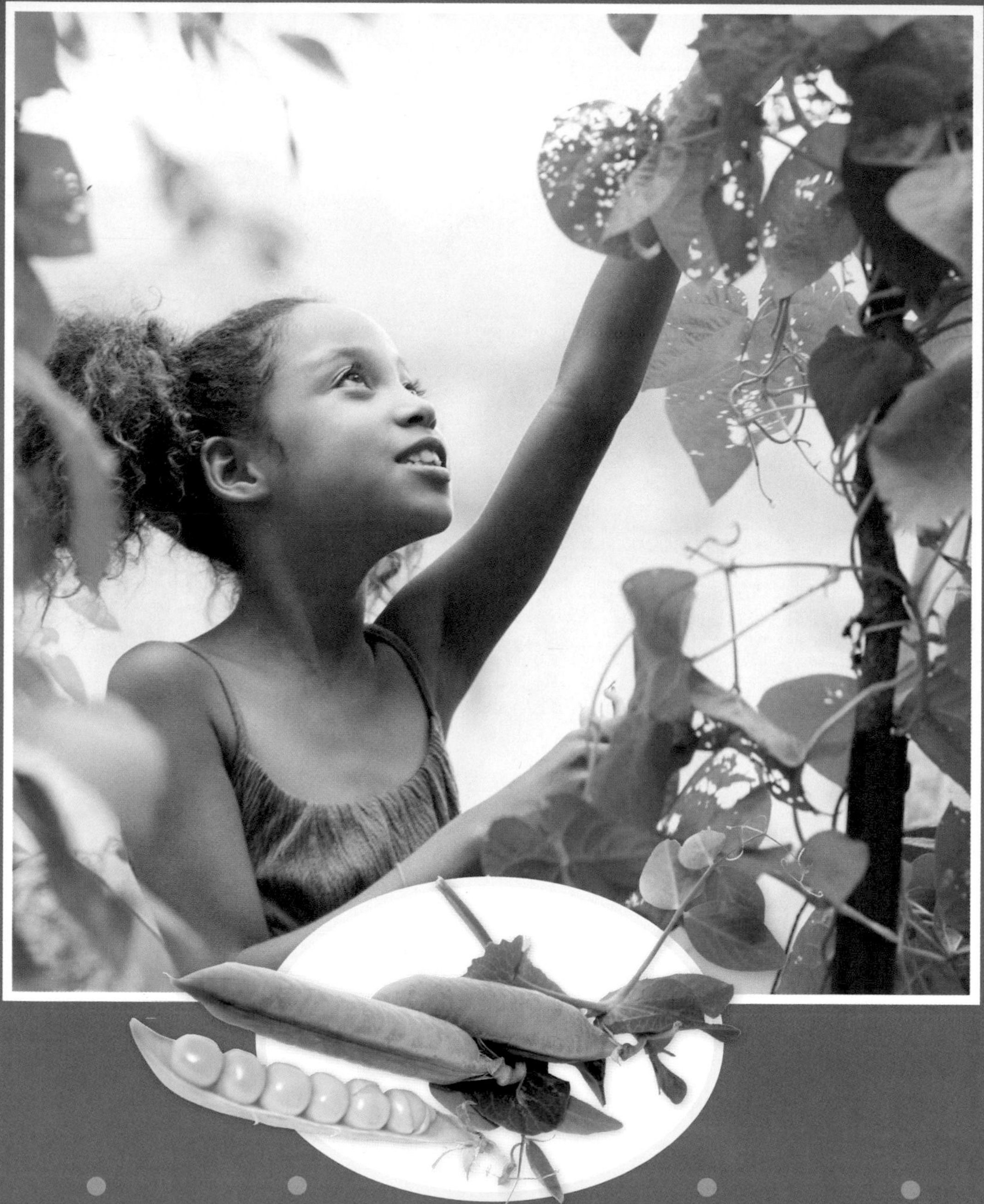

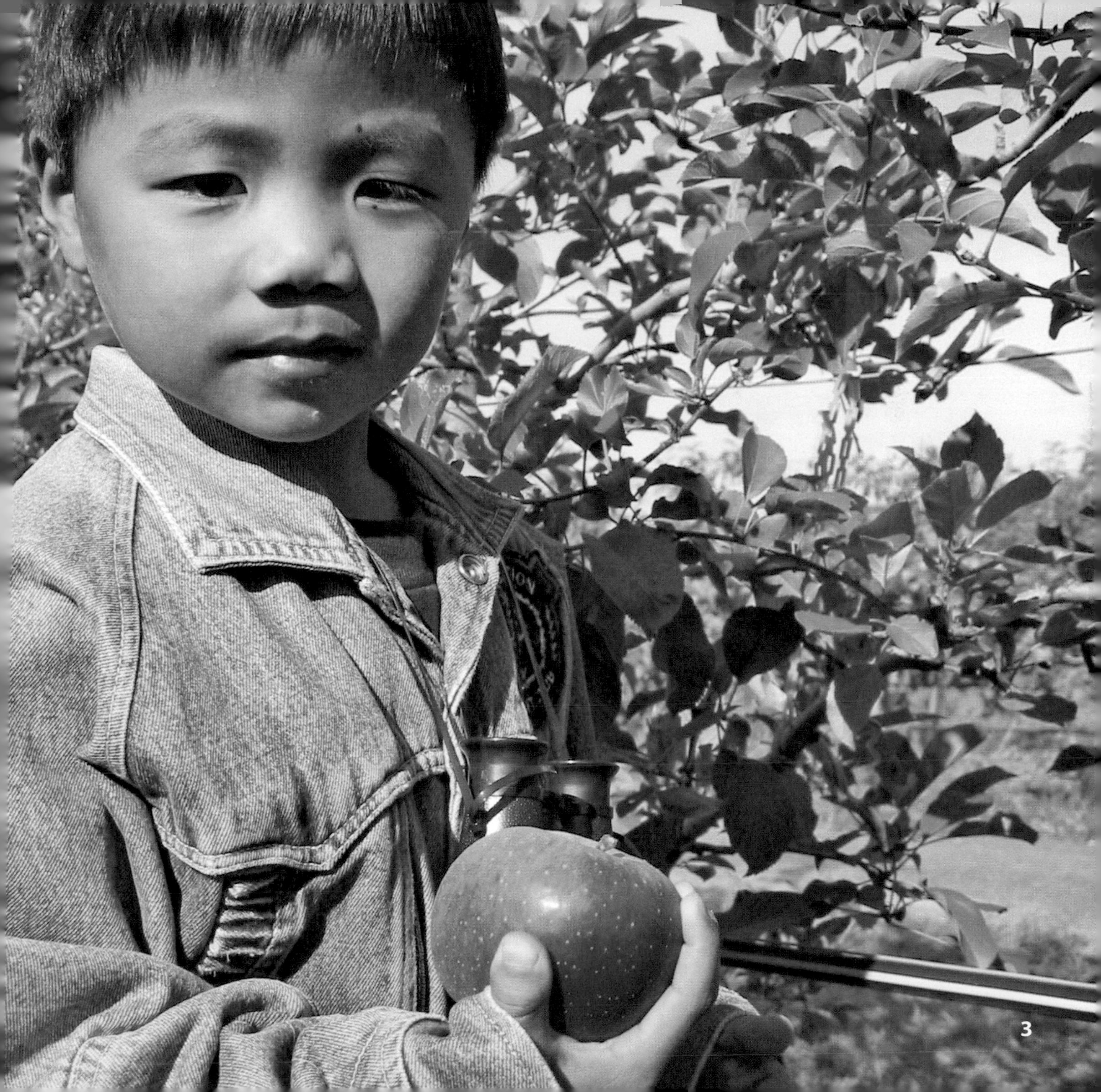

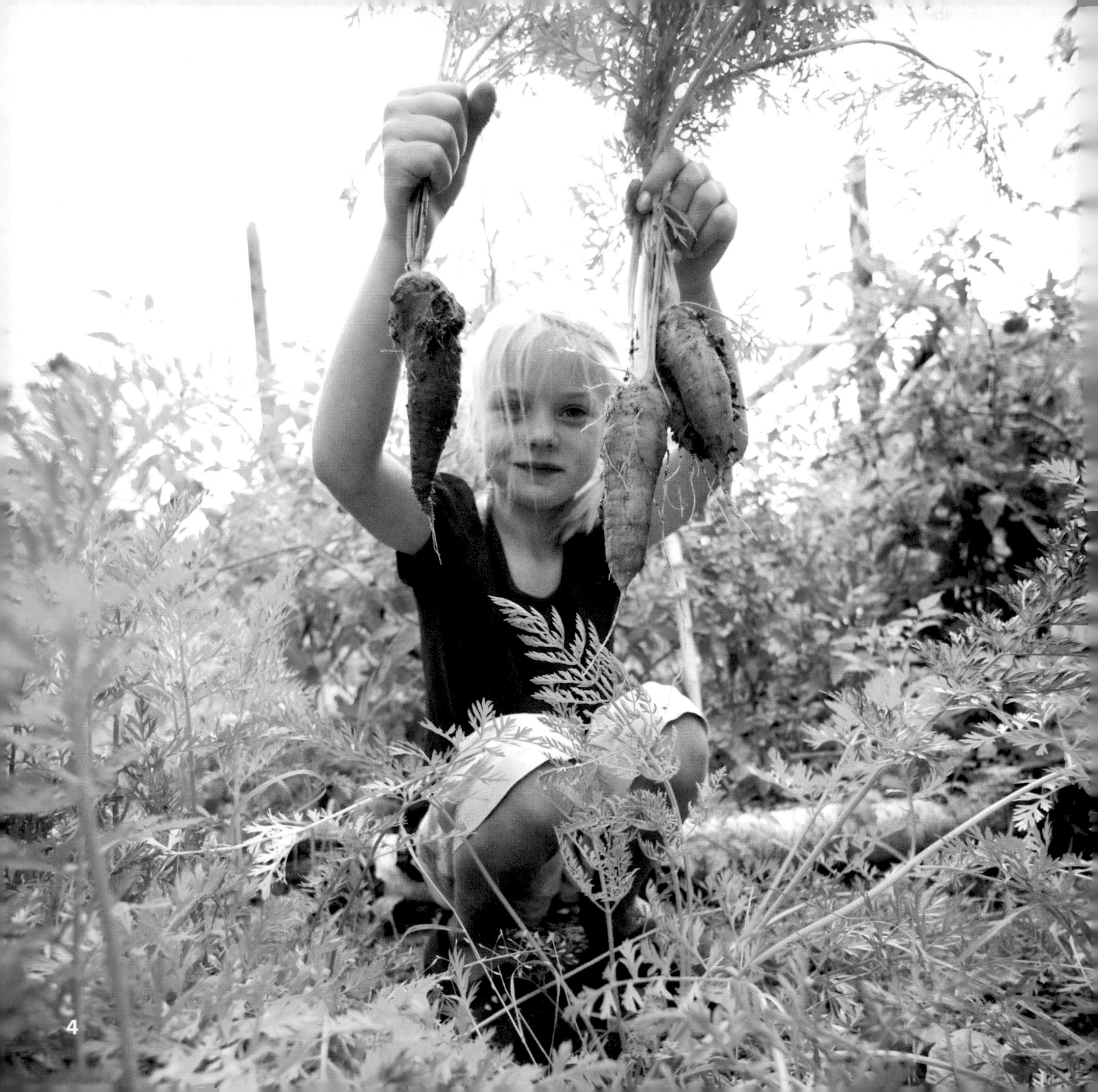

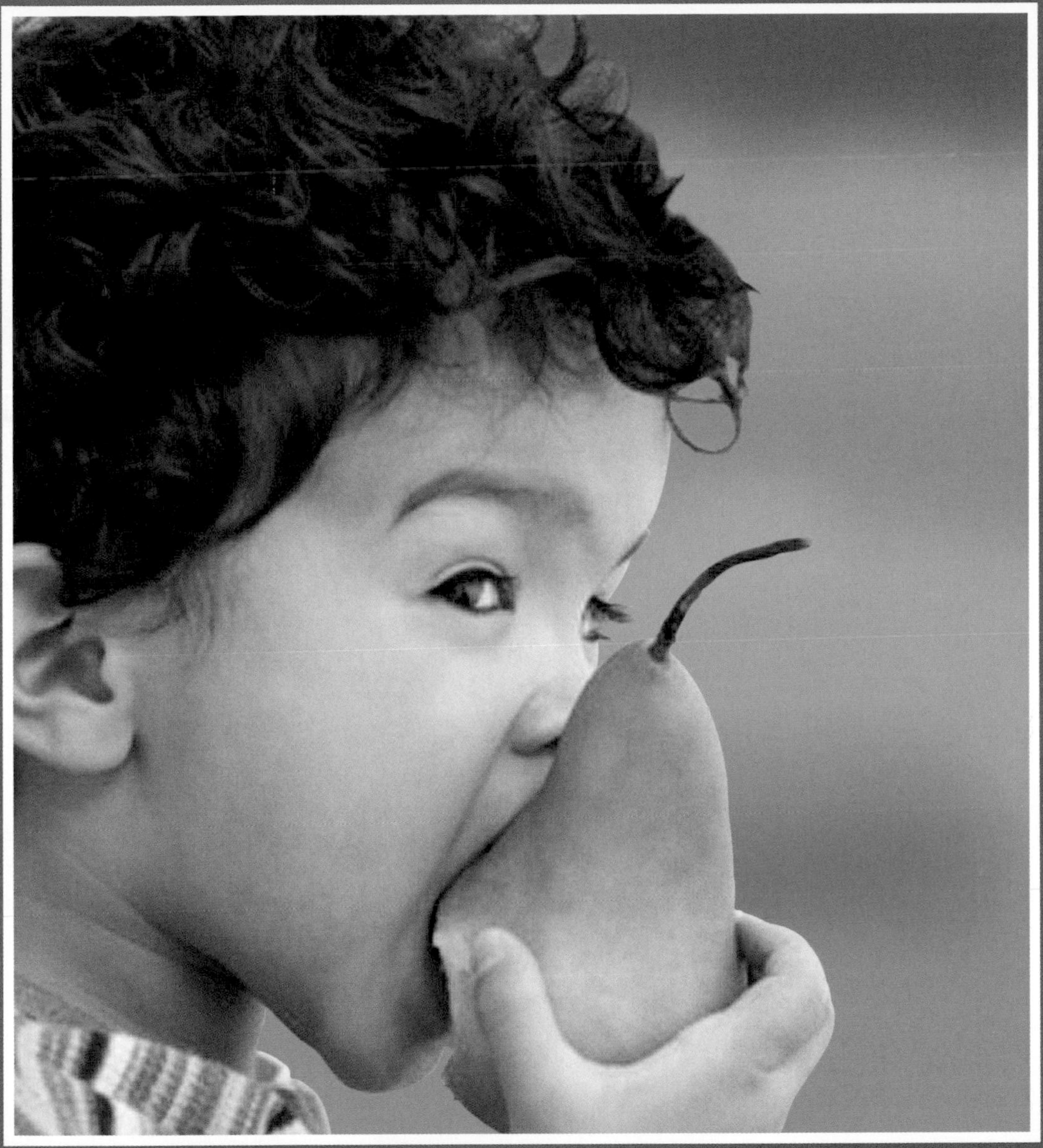

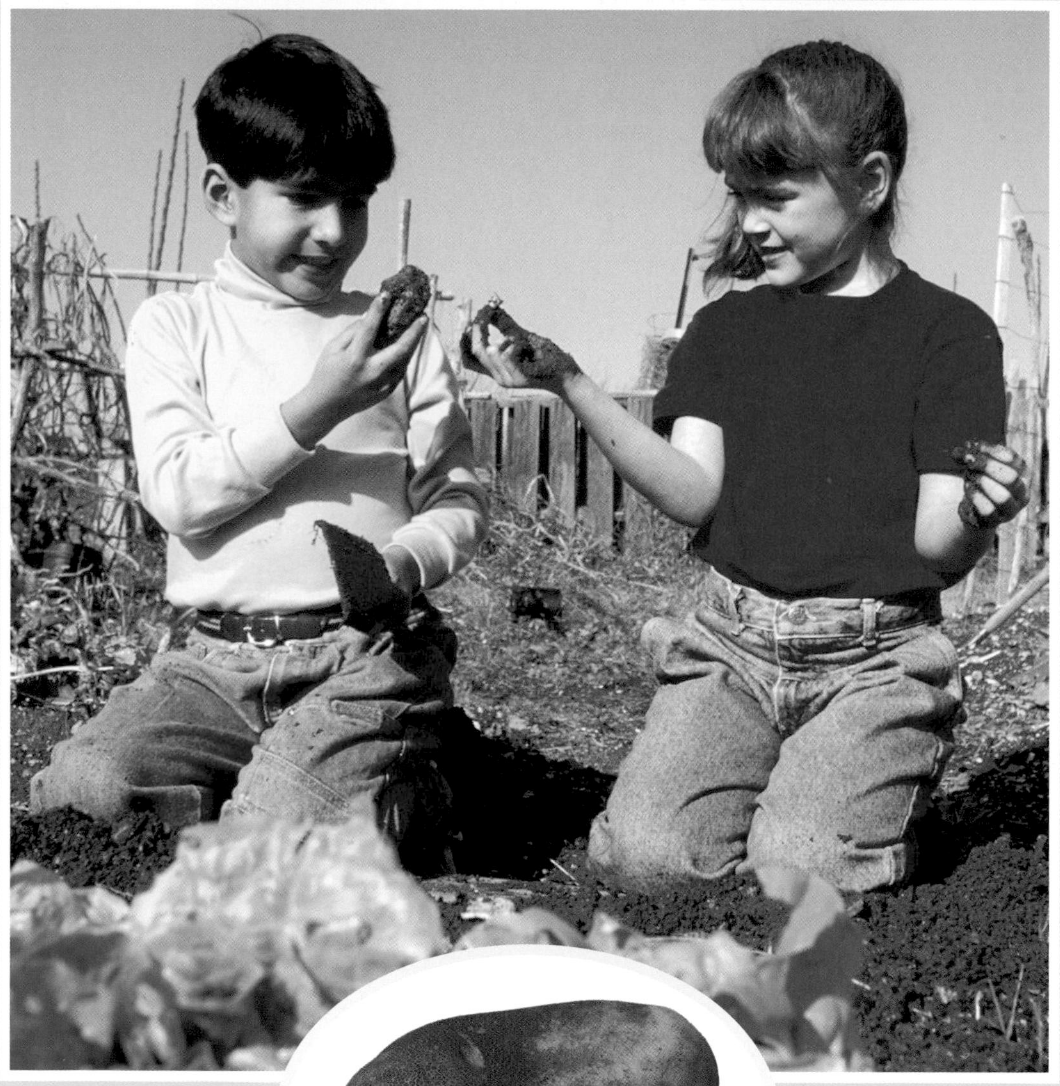

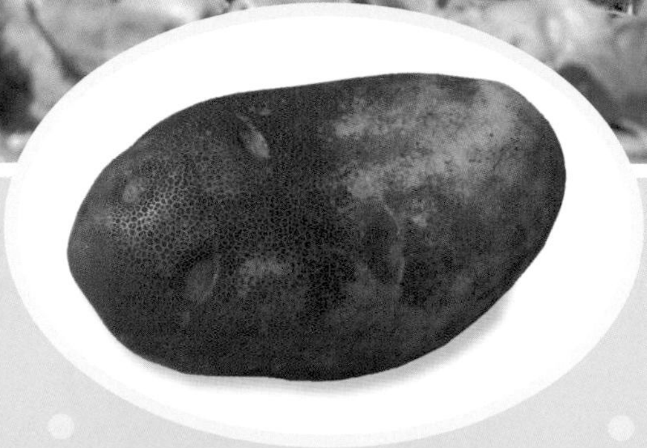

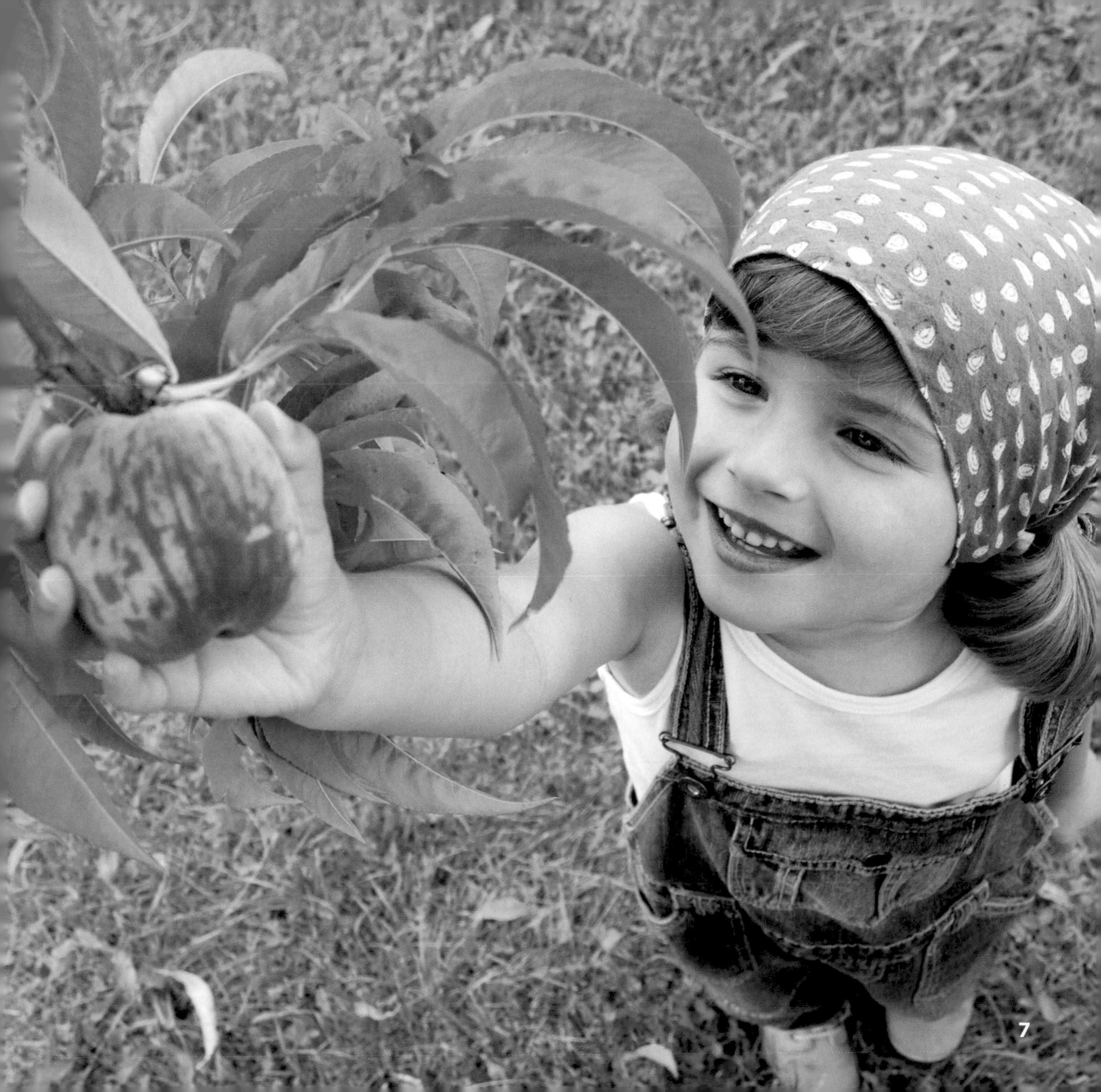

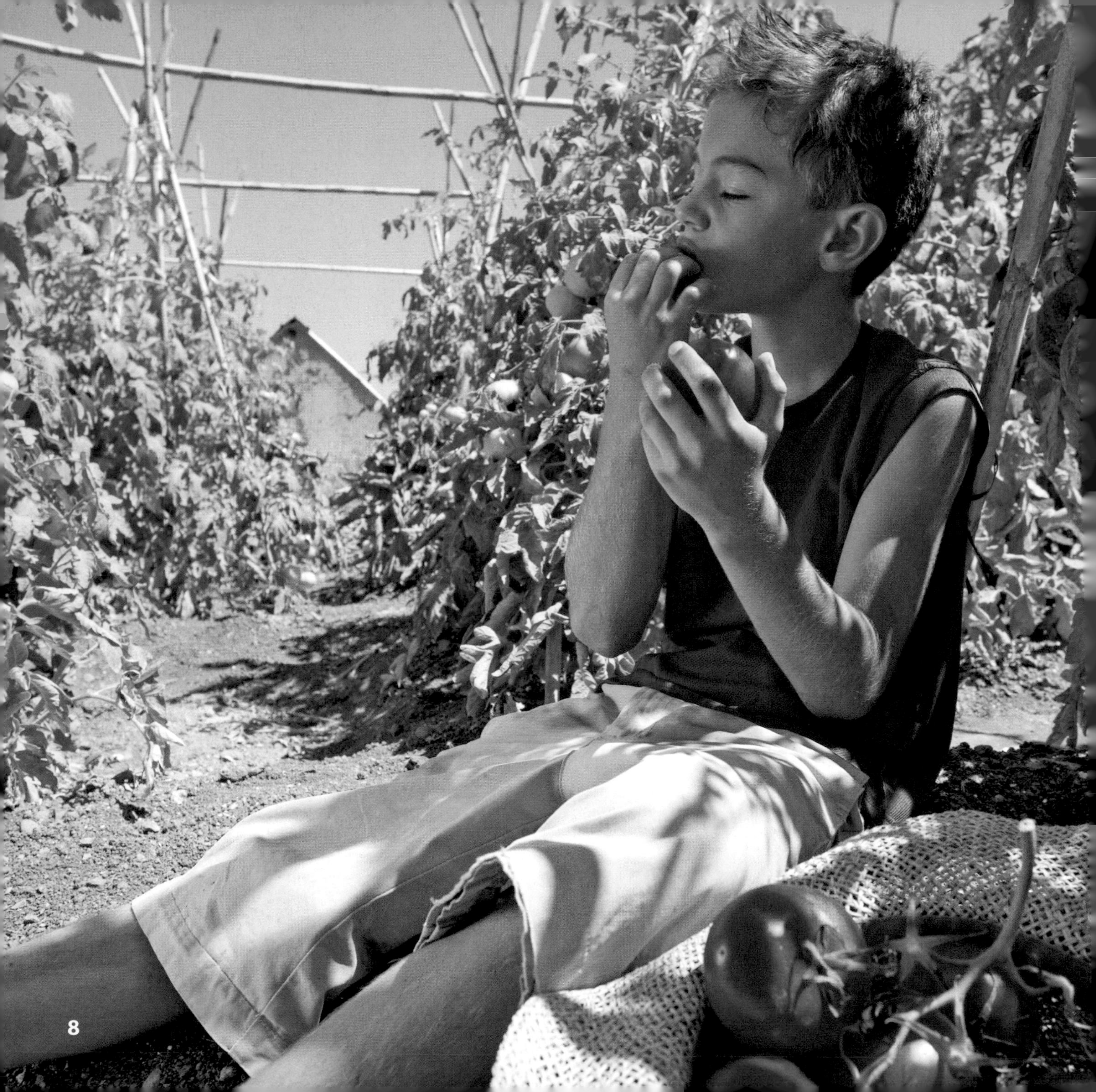